DATA VISUALIZATION

FOR BEGINNERS

LEARN TO DESIGN, INTERPRET, AND OPTIMIZE 40+ ESSENTIAL CHARTS

VIVIAN HART

TABLE OF CONTENTS

INTRODUCTION

Why This Book is a Game Changer for You

Imagine walking into a meeting, armed with data that could change the direction of your company, project, or research. You've spent hours—maybe even days—gathering insights, analyzing numbers, and preparing your argument. But as you begin to present, you see glazed eyes, furrowed brows, and distracted glances. Your audience is lost. Your data is **powerful**, but without the right visualization, it fails to tell the story you want it to tell.

Now, imagine a different scenario. You present your data using the **right** charts, colors, and layouts. Instead of confusion, you see **engagement**. People lean in, nodding in understanding. Your insights are **immediately clear**, and your audience grasps your message **at a glance**. You don't need to convince them—your visuals do the work for you.

This is the power of **effective data visualization**, and it's exactly what this book is here to teach you. Whether you're a complete beginner or someone looking to sharpen your skills, this guide will take you from **basic charts** to **compelling, story-driven visuals** that **influence, persuade, and clarify**.

1

Why Data Visualization Matters

We live in a world overflowing with data. From business reports and marketing analytics to scientific studies and financial trends, **data is everywhere**. But raw numbers and spreadsheets **alone** don't drive decisions—**understanding them does**.

The truth is, the human brain is not built to process large volumes of numbers efficiently. **We are visual creatures.**Studies show that people remember:

65% of visual content compared to only **10-20% of text-based information**

Information presented with **relevant visuals** is processed **60,000 times faster** than text alone

Decision-makers are **twice as likely** to act on data that is clearly visualized

This means that if you're presenting data—whether in a business meeting, a classroom, or an online report—how you **display** your information is just as important as the data itself.

Poor data visualization can lead to:

- Misinterpretation of key insights
- Loss of engagement from your audience

- Poor decision-making due to unclear messaging

But when done right, data visualization can:

Simplify complexity—turning raw data into clear insights

Enhance engagement—keeping your audience focused and interested

Drive action—helping people make informed, confident decisions

This book will show you **exactly how** to achieve that.

The Psychology Behind Effective Visuals

Why do some charts immediately make sense while others feel confusing? Why do certain colors **grab attention**, while others get ignored?

The secret lies in **visual perception**—how our brains **naturally** process and interpret images. Understanding a few key principles can **drastically improve** how you present your data.

1. The Brain Loves Patterns

Our brains are wired to **find patterns and relationships** in visual data. That's why trends in a **line chart** are easier to recognize than a table full of numbers. We **see** the movement and direction without effort.

Tip: When showing trends, **use line charts**, **area charts**, or **slope charts** rather than raw tables.

2. Color Impacts Interpretation

Colors do more than just make visuals look pretty—they **guide attention** and **evoke emotions**.

Red = Urgency, Warning, Decline
Green = Growth, Success, Positive Trends
Blue = Trust, Stability, Business Reports
Yellow = Caution, Highlights

Tip: Use **color strategically**—don't overload your charts with unnecessary hues. Stick to **one or two highlight colors** to emphasize key data points.

3. Simplicity Beats Complexity

Have you ever looked at a chart **so overloaded with information** that it made your brain hurt? **Clutter kills comprehension.**

Tip: Stick to the **"less is more"** rule: **remove unnecessary gridlines, labels, and excessive details**. Your goal is **clarity, not decoration**.

4. The Right Chart Tells the Right Story

Not all charts are created equal. **Using the wrong one can completely mislead your audience.**

A pie chart with **too many slices**? Confusing.
A simple **bar chart** for comparisons? Much better.

This book will help you **choose the right chart every time**.

Choosing the Right Chart for Your Data

One of the biggest mistakes people make in data visualization is **picking the wrong chart type**. A poorly chosen chart can **distort the message, confuse the audience**, or even **lead to the wrong conclusions**.

Here's a quick breakdown of **when to use different chart types**:

1. Showing Trends Over Time

Best Charts: Line Charts, Area Charts, Slope Charts
Avoid: Pie Charts (they don't show trends!)

2. Comparing Categories or Groups

Best Charts: Bar Charts, Column Charts, Bullet Charts
Avoid: 3D Charts (they distort data and are hard to read)

3. Displaying Distributions

Best Charts: Histograms, Box Plots, Violin Plots
Avoid: Pie Charts (they don't show distribution at all)

4. Showing Relationships & Correlations

Best Charts: Scatter Plots, Bubble Charts, Heatmaps
Avoid: Line Charts (they don't show correlation effectively)

By the time you finish this book, you'll know exactly **which chart to choose** based on the message you want to convey.

Common Pitfalls & How to Avoid Them

Even experienced professionals make mistakes in data visualization. Here are some of the most common **errors to watch out for**:

1. Overloading with Too Much Data

Fix: Keep your charts simple—**focus on key takeaways, not every data point**.

2. Using the Wrong Scale

Fix: Ensure your **axes are proportional** and avoid **truncated scales that mislead viewers**.

3. Misusing Pie Charts

Fix: Use **pie charts only when comparing a few categories—** otherwise, switch to a bar chart.

4. Ignoring Accessibility

Fix: Ensure **colorblind-friendly palettes** and provide **clear labels** for all charts.

This book will **walk you through these mistakes in detail**, with before-and-after examples so you **never make them again**.

Why You Need This Book

There are **many books** on data visualization—but **here's why this one is different**:

- **Beginner-Friendly:** No prior experience? No problem. This book explains everything in **simple, easy-to-follow language**.
- **Practical & Actionable:** Step-by-step guidance with **real-world examples** and **hands-on exercises**.
- **Covers the Latest Trends:** Learn **modern visualization techniques** beyond basic charts.

- **Avoids Common Mistakes:** See **before-and-after chart redesigns** to instantly improve your visuals.
- **Great for Any Industry:** Whether you're in **business, marketing, finance, research, or education**, this book will **help you create compelling visuals**.

By the time you finish, you'll be able to **transform boring charts into powerful visual stories**, communicate data **clearly and effectively**, and **stand out** in presentations, reports, and dashboards.

What's Next?

Now that you understand **why data visualization is so important**, it's time to dive in. In the next chapter, we'll **break down the fundamentals** of creating visuals that are **not only clear but also engaging and persuasive**.

Ready to start? Let's go!

1.

FUNDAMENTALS OF DATA VISUALIZATION

How the Brain Processes Visual Information

Data visualization is not just about making numbers look appealing—it's about **communication**. The way information is presented can mean the difference between clarity and confusion, engagement and disinterest, or even success and failure in decision-making.

At its core, effective data visualization leverages how the human brain **naturally** processes information. Unlike raw numbers in a spreadsheet, visual representations of data allow people to **grasp patterns, trends, and insights almost instantly**.

The Science Behind Visual Processing

The human brain is wired to process images far more efficiently than text or numbers. Research shows that:

- The brain **processes visual information 60,000 times faster** than text.

- People **remember 65% of visual content** three days later, compared to just 10-20% of text-based information.
- Visuals account for **90% of the information** transmitted to the brain.

This is why an effective chart or graph can communicate a complex idea **in seconds**, while a table full of numbers requires careful analysis.

Pattern Recognition: The Key to Quick Insights

One of the most powerful aspects of visual perception is **pattern recognition**. The brain is constantly looking for relationships between elements—**trends, clusters, outliers, and comparisons**. This is why:

- **Line charts** make trends over time immediately recognizable.
- **Bar charts** allow for quick comparisons between categories.
- **Heatmaps** help identify patterns in large datasets through color variations.

By aligning visualizations with **how the brain naturally seeks information**, you can create charts and graphics that are not only clear but **memorable and persuasive**.

Key Visual Variables and Their Impact

Every data visualization relies on a few **core visual elements** to convey meaning. These elements—when used correctly—can **enhance comprehension**. When misused, they can distort data and **lead to misinterpretation**.

1. Position

Position is one of the most powerful ways to represent data because the human eye **quickly detects differences in spatial arrangement**. For example:

- **Scatter plots** use position on an x-y plane to reveal correlations between two variables.
- **Bar charts** arrange bars along a common baseline, making height differences easy to compare.

2. Length

The length of an element is crucial for communicating quantitative differences. This is why **bar charts are more effective than pie charts**—our brains compare lengths more accurately than angles.

3. Color

Color enhances data interpretation, but it must be used with purpose. It can:

- **Differentiate categories** (e.g., product types, regions, or teams).
- **Highlight important insights** (e.g., using red for a drop in sales).
- **Show intensity or distribution** (e.g., heatmaps).

However, too many colors can overwhelm and confuse the audience. Consistency and **color accessibility** (considering colorblind-friendly palettes) are essential.

4. Shape

Shapes are particularly useful in scatter plots and network diagrams. They can:

- **Differentiate categories** when multiple datasets overlap.
- **Help in legend-free design**, where shapes alone indicate data groups.

5. Size

Size is often used to represent magnitude, such as in **bubble charts** where the size of each circle corresponds to a data value. However, size differences should be used with caution—people often **misjudge** relative area sizes, leading to potential misinterpretation.

6. Orientation

The direction of an element can change how data is perceived. For example:

- **Slope charts** use orientation to show shifts in data over time.
- **Arrow-based flow diagrams** visually represent movement or change.

When choosing a visualization, ensuring that these variables are used **intuitively and effectively** will determine how well your audience understands the message.

The Four Golden Rules of Effective Visualization

1. Keep It Simple

One of the most common mistakes in data visualization is **overcomplicating the design**. While it's tempting to include multiple effects, 3D elements, and excessive labels, **simplicity is key**.

A clear, straightforward chart allows viewers to focus on **the message, not the design itself**. This means:

- Avoid unnecessary gridlines, shading, and decorative elements.
- Use **minimal but clear labels**—don't clutter the visualization.
- Stick to **one or two highlight colors** to guide attention.

2. Choose the Right Chart Type

Not all charts serve the same purpose. Using the wrong one can **mislead your audience** or make your insights harder to interpret.

- **Use line charts for trends over time** (not pie charts).
- **Use bar charts for comparisons** (not multiple pie charts).
- **Use scatter plots for correlations** (not line charts).

A well-chosen chart type **amplifies your data's meaning** instead of distorting it.

3. Use Consistent Scales and Avoid Distortion

A misleading scale can **completely change the interpretation of data**. Consider these examples:

- A **bar chart with a truncated y-axis** (not starting at zero) can exaggerate differences.
- A **distorted aspect ratio on a line chart** can make fluctuations seem more dramatic than they are.

- A **pie chart with unequal segment colors** may create an unintended emphasis.

Maintaining **proportionality and consistency** is critical to ensure that your data remains **honest and accurate**.

4. Focus on the Story, Not Just the Data

Great data visualization is more than just charts and numbers—it's about **telling a story**. A well-structured visualization answers these key questions:

- **What is the main takeaway?**
- **What action should the viewer take?**
- **How does this data fit into the bigger picture?**

A well-designed chart **guides the viewer through the data** naturally, leading them toward the key insight **without confusion**.

Storytelling with Data: Making an Impact

Data by itself **does not engage**. A spreadsheet full of numbers may contain powerful insights, but without a compelling **narrative**, it's just raw information.

Why Storytelling Matters

When data is presented in **story format**, people are:

- **More likely to retain the information.**
- **More engaged and emotionally connected.**
- **More persuaded by the insights presented.**

Storytelling in data visualization involves:

1. **Setting the Stage:** Provide context—what problem are we solving?
2. **Introducing the Data:** Show the trends, comparisons, or insights clearly.
3. **Building to the Key Message:** Highlight the **most important** takeaway.
4. **Closing with Actionable Insights:** What should the audience **do** with this information?

Example: The Power of Narrative in Data

Let's say you're presenting sales performance for the past year. Instead of just showing a **static bar chart**, you could structure it as a story:

- **Beginning:** "Sales were stable in Q1 and Q2, with moderate growth."
- **Middle:** "In Q3, we see a dramatic spike—what happened?" (Show a sharp increase in the line chart.)

- **End:** "Q4 performance dipped—this was due to lower holiday promotions. Here's how we can improve next year."

This simple approach **transforms data into an actionable insight**, rather than just numbers on a chart.

Final Thoughts

Mastering the fundamentals of data visualization is **not just about charts—it's about communication**. By understanding how the brain processes information, using key visual variables effectively, and following the **golden rules of clarity, consistency, and storytelling**, you can **turn raw data into meaningful insights**.

In the next chapter, we'll dive into **how to visualize trends over time**, covering the best charts and techniques to ensure your data is both compelling and easy to understand.

2.

VISUALIZING CHANGE OVER TIME (TRACKING TRENDS & PATTERNS)

In today's fast-paced world, data is constantly in motion. Whether you are monitoring stock prices, tracking website traffic, or managing a project timeline, understanding how data changes over time is crucial. Visualizing these changes allows you to see trends, detect patterns, and even predict future developments. In this chapter, we will explore several powerful tools for visualizing change over time. We will examine line charts, fan charts, slope charts, area charts, connected scatterplots, and Gantt charts—each offering unique advantages for different types of time-based data. By the end of this chapter, you will be equipped with the knowledge to choose the right visualization for your specific needs, helping you transform raw data into actionable insights.

Introduction: The Importance of Visualizing Change Over Time

Data that evolves over time carries a story. It tells us not only where we are, but also how we arrived there and where we might be headed. Whether you're a business leader making strategic decisions, a researcher tracking experimental outcomes, or a project manager coordinating timelines, understanding trends and patterns is essential. Time-series data is inherently dynamic, and traditional static representations such as tables can obscure the narrative that unfolds over days, months, or years.

Visualizing change over time can reveal seasonality, cyclic behavior, and unexpected trends. It can highlight periods of growth or decline and provide context to the fluctuations. With effective visualizations, complex data becomes accessible and understandable, even to audiences without a technical background. In the sections that follow, we will explore several chart types designed specifically for tracking change over time. Each type offers its own perspective, helping you to tell a complete and compelling story.

Line Charts: When & How to Use Them

Line charts are one of the most widely recognized and frequently used methods for representing time-series data. They connect data points with a continuous line, providing a clear visual representation of trends and patterns over a continuous interval.

Here's the first graph, a **Line Chart** showing stock prices over a year.

Why Use Line Charts?

Line charts are ideal when you want to:

- **Show Trends:** They provide an immediate sense of whether values are increasing, decreasing, or remaining stable over time.
- **Depict Continuity:** By connecting the dots, line charts emphasize the continuity of data, which is essential when the data points are part of a sequential series.
- **Compare Multiple Series:** When comparing different datasets over the same time period, multiple lines can be

drawn on the same chart. This makes it easy to see how different variables relate to one another.

Best Practices for Creating Effective Line Charts

1. **Keep It Simple:**
    Ensure that the chart is not cluttered. If multiple lines are necessary, use different colors or line styles that are distinct yet harmonious. Avoid excessive gridlines or distracting markers unless they add meaningful context.

2. **Label Clearly:**
    Axes should be clearly labeled with appropriate units of measurement, and each line should have a legend to indicate what it represents. Use consistent intervals for the time axis to maintain clarity.

3. **Highlight Key Points:**
    Consider annotating critical data points or periods of significant change. This could be done by adding text annotations or using a contrasting color to draw attention.

4. **Mind the Scale:**
    Ensure that the scale of the y-axis accurately reflects the range of your data. A poorly chosen scale can either exaggerate or minimize trends, leading to misinterpretation.

Common Use Cases

- **Financial Data:** Tracking stock prices or revenue over time.
- **Website Analytics:** Showing trends in visitor numbers or engagement metrics.
- **Scientific Research:** Charting experimental results or measurements over sequential time points.

By following these guidelines, you can harness the power of line charts to create clear, compelling visualizations that capture the essence of your data's journey through time.

Fan Charts: Visualizing Uncertainty

While line charts are excellent for depicting trends, they often do not account for uncertainty. In many scenarios—especially forecasting or predictive modeling—it's crucial to show not only a central estimate but also the range of possible outcomes. This is where fan charts come in.

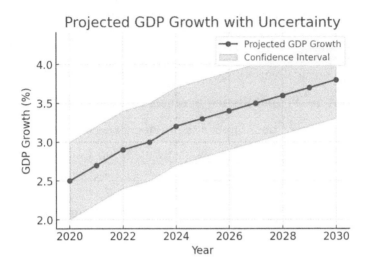

Here's the **Fan Chart**, showing projected GDP growth with a confidence interval to represent uncertainty.

Understanding Fan Charts

Fan charts are designed to display a central forecast along with varying degrees of uncertainty around it. They do this by using a series of shaded bands, each representing a different probability interval. The resulting "fan" of color allows viewers to understand the confidence associated with the central estimate.

Why Use Fan Charts?

Fan charts are particularly useful when you need to:

- **Communicate Uncertainty:** They visually convey the range within which future data points may fall, based on historical variability or model predictions.
- **Show Probabilistic Forecasts:** Instead of a single, definitive line, fan charts provide a spectrum of outcomes, which is especially useful in economic forecasting or weather prediction.
- **Enhance Decision-Making:** By presenting the uncertainty, decision-makers can weigh risks more effectively and plan for multiple scenarios.

Best Practices for Creating Fan Charts

1. **Choose Meaningful Intervals:**
   Define the probability intervals that are most relevant to your audience. Common intervals might include 50%, 75%, and 95% confidence levels. Clearly indicate these on the chart so that viewers understand what each band represents.
2. **Use a Consistent Color Gradient:**
   Select a color gradient that becomes lighter or less saturated as uncertainty increases. This visual cue helps the viewer intuitively grasp that the outer bands are less certain.
3. **Avoid Overcomplication:**
   While fan charts provide more information than simple

line charts, it is important not to overwhelm the viewer. Ensure that the chart remains clear by limiting the number of bands and using clear labels.

4. **Provide Context:**
    Explain in accompanying text or a legend what the different bands represent. Clarify how the uncertainty was calculated and why it matters.

Common Use Cases

- **Economic Forecasts:** Central banks and financial institutions use fan charts to predict future economic indicators such as inflation or GDP growth.
- **Weather Predictions:** Meteorologists use fan charts to represent the range of possible temperature or precipitation outcomes.
- **Project Forecasting:** In project management, fan charts can illustrate the range of possible completion dates based on historical data.

By using fan charts, you add an important layer of depth to your time-based visualizations, acknowledging that the future is not set in stone and that uncertainty is an inherent part of prediction.

Slope Charts: Comparing Changes Between Two Points

When you need to make direct comparisons between two distinct points in time, slope charts are an excellent tool. They are particularly effective when you want to highlight the magnitude of change for various categories or groups between two moments.

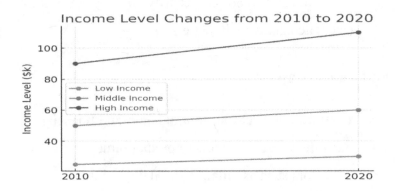

Here's the **Slope Chart**, comparing income levels in 2010 and 2020.

Why Use Slope Charts?

Slope charts are best suited for:

- **Before-and-After Comparisons:** They allow you to see how values have changed between two time periods, making them ideal for illustrating the impact of a specific event or policy change.

- **Highlighting Differences Across Categories:** By drawing a line for each category, slope charts make it easy to compare the rate of change between them.
- **Simplicity and Clarity:** Unlike more complex time-series charts, slope charts distill the information down to a single change per category, reducing visual clutter.

Designing Effective Slope Charts

1. **Select Two Key Time Points:**
   Choose the two moments that are most significant to your analysis. This could be the beginning and end of a fiscal year, before and after a major campaign, or any other relevant points in time.
2. **Ensure Consistent Scales:**
   The axis should be consistent to allow for accurate comparison. Misleading scales can exaggerate or diminish the apparent change between the two points.
3. **Use Clear Labels and Annotations:**
   Each line should be clearly labeled with its corresponding category, and it can be helpful to annotate significant shifts. Adding numerical values at the endpoints can further clarify the magnitude of change.
4. **Minimize Clutter:**
   Since slope charts are designed to compare only two points, avoid adding unnecessary elements that could

distract from the main message. Keep the design minimal and focused.

Common Use Cases

- **Educational Data:** Comparing test scores before and after a new teaching method.
- **Sales Performance:** Illustrating the change in sales figures before and after a marketing campaign.
- **Policy Impact:** Demonstrating the effect of regulatory changes on key performance indicators.

By emphasizing the direct change between two points, slope charts provide a straightforward way to convey the direction and magnitude of change. They are an invaluable tool when your goal is to make clear, concise comparisons without the distraction of extraneous data.

Area Charts: Emphasizing Volume & Trends

Area charts build on the foundation of line charts by filling the area beneath the line with color. This technique not only illustrates trends over time but also emphasizes the magnitude or volume of the data. Area charts can be used to depict both individual series and cumulative totals, offering a visually rich method for displaying data trends.

Why Use Area Charts?

Area charts are particularly useful when you want to:

- **Highlight Cumulative Data:** The filled area draws attention to the overall volume, making it easy to see how a total accumulates over time.
- **Depict Trends with Emphasis:** The visual weight of the colored area reinforces the importance of the trend and can make subtle changes more apparent.
- **Show Multiple Data Series:** Stacked area charts, in particular, allow you to visualize the contribution of each component to the whole, which is ideal for understanding how different segments evolve over time.

Best Practices for Creating Area Charts

1. **Choose Appropriate Color Schemes:**
   Use colors that are distinct yet harmonious, ensuring that each area is easily distinguishable. When stacking multiple series, choose a palette that maintains clarity and avoids visual confusion.
2. **Ensure Proper Ordering:**
   In stacked area charts, the order of the layers matters. Arrange the data so that the most important or largest

values are positioned in a way that does not obscure smaller trends.

3. **Label Clearly:**

Like other charts, ensure that both axes are labeled and that each area is identified. Consider using legends or annotations to clarify what each area represents.

4. **Mind the Baseline:**

The baseline (usually zero) is crucial for interpreting the data correctly. Ensure that the area chart accurately reflects the volume without misleading exaggeration or minimization.

Common Use Cases

- **Cumulative Sales Data:** Displaying how total sales accumulate over time, with different product lines represented in a stacked area chart.
- **Website Analytics:** Showing how total visits or page views build up over time, with various traffic sources differentiated by color.
- **Financial Data:** Illustrating how different revenue streams contribute to overall revenue growth throughout the year.

By using area charts effectively, you can emphasize not only the trend of your data but also the scale of change. This dual focus on trend and volume makes area charts a versatile tool for storytelling in time-series data visualization.

Connected Scatterplots: Showing Relationships Over Time

Connected scatterplots offer a unique way to visualize data that evolves over time by combining elements of both scatterplots and line charts. In a connected scatterplot, individual data points are plotted on a scatter diagram and then connected in the order of their occurrence, thus revealing both the relationship between variables and their progression over time.

Why Use Connected Scatterplots?

Connected scatterplots are ideal for scenarios where you need to:

- **Show Dual Relationships:** They allow you to explore the relationship between two variables while also incorporating a time dimension.
- **Illustrate Dynamic Interactions:** By connecting the points, you can see how the relationship between the variables changes over time.
- **Reveal Patterns and Cycles:** The connected lines can help uncover cyclical behavior or gradual shifts that may be less apparent in a static scatterplot.

Design Considerations for Connected Scatterplots

1. **Select Meaningful Variables:**
   Identify the two variables that have an important or interesting relationship. The x-axis and y-axis should represent dimensions that interact in a way that is insightful when tracked over time.

2. **Use Distinct Markers and Lines:**
   Differentiate between the data points and the connecting lines. The points themselves can be highlighted with markers, while the lines should be subtle enough to indicate continuity without overwhelming the scatter plot.

3. **Annotate Key Time Points:**
   Include annotations or markers for significant dates or events that might explain shifts in the relationship between the variables.

4. **Maintain a Logical Order:**
   Ensure that the connection of points follows a logical time sequence. If the data is not sequentially ordered, the connected scatterplot will not accurately represent the evolution of the relationship.

Common Use Cases

- **Economic Indicators:** For instance, a connected scatterplot can be used to illustrate the relationship between unemployment and inflation over time, highlighting the dynamic interplay between these variables.

- **Health Metrics:** Tracking how changes in one health metric (like body weight) relate to another (such as blood pressure) over a period can provide valuable insights into health trends.

- **Environmental Studies:** Visualizing how temperature and humidity interact over time can help in understanding climate patterns and weather dynamics.

Connected scatterplots bring a dual layer of insight—both the correlation between two variables and their progression through time. This duality makes them a powerful tool for nuanced data analysis.

Gantt Charts: Tracking Project Timelines

Gantt charts hold a special place in the realm of data visualization because they focus not on quantitative data per se, but on the sequencing and scheduling of tasks. Widely used in project management, Gantt charts offer a clear overview of project timelines, task durations, and dependencies, making them indispensable for planning and execution.

Why Use Gantt Charts?

Gantt charts are designed to help you:

- **Visualize Project Schedules:** They provide a clear timeline of tasks, showing start and end dates for each component of a project.
- **Manage Dependencies:** By displaying which tasks must be completed before others can begin, Gantt charts help you understand the project's critical path.
- **Monitor Progress:** As tasks are completed, Gantt charts can be updated to reflect current progress, enabling real-time tracking of project status.
- **Facilitate Communication:** They serve as a communication tool for team members, stakeholders, and managers, ensuring that everyone is aware of deadlines and responsibilities.

Designing an Effective Gantt Chart

1. **List All Tasks:**
   Start by breaking down the project into all its constituent tasks. Each task should be clearly defined with a start date, end date, and duration.
2. **Establish Dependencies:**
   Determine which tasks depend on others. Use connecting lines or arrows to indicate these dependencies clearly.
3. **Choose a Clear Layout:**
   Arrange tasks in a logical order along the vertical axis and use the horizontal axis to represent time. Ensure that

the time intervals are consistent and that the chart is easy to read at a glance.

4. **Update Regularly:**

A Gantt chart is only as useful as it is current. Regularly update the chart to reflect progress, delays, or changes in the project timeline.

Common Use Cases

- **Construction Projects:** Coordinating multiple phases of construction, from planning and permits to execution and final inspections.
- **Software Development:** Tracking sprints, milestones, and release dates, ensuring that development teams stay on schedule.
- **Marketing Campaigns:** Organizing the timeline for campaign launch, content creation, media placements, and performance review.

Gantt charts translate the complexity of project timelines into a simple, visual format. They allow you to see the big picture at a glance and drill down into specific details when necessary, making them an essential tool for any project-driven endeavor.

Conclusion: Harnessing Time to Tell Your Story

Visualizing change over time is more than just plotting numbers on a chart—it is about capturing the essence of a journey. From the clarity of line charts that show straightforward trends, to the nuanced representation of uncertainty with fan charts, and from the direct comparisons enabled by slope charts to the rich narratives in area charts and connected scatterplots, each visualization tool has a distinct role to play.

Gantt charts remind us that not all data is about numbers; some data tells the story of processes, projects, and plans. Together, these tools empower you to convey your data's narrative with precision, clarity, and impact.

By understanding when and how to use each of these visualizations, you can transform your time-series data into a compelling story that guides your audience through the past, present, and future of your information. This not only helps in decision-making but also in communicating complex ideas in a way that is engaging and accessible.

As you continue your journey in data visualization, keep in mind that the goal is always to inform, persuade, and inspire action. Every chart, every graph, and every timeline is a tool in your arsenal to make data come alive. The techniques and best practices discussed in this chapter are designed to help you choose the right visualization for the right situation, ensuring that your data not only tells a story but tells it well.

Take these insights and apply them to your own projects. Experiment with different chart types, tailor your designs to your audience's needs, and always strive for clarity and simplicity. Remember that effective visualization is an iterative process—each time you create a new chart, you learn more about how to better communicate your message.

In the next chapter, we will delve into another critical aspect of data visualization, exploring how to compare and rank data effectively. For now, let this chapter serve as your guide to mastering the art of visualizing change over time, so that every trend, every pattern, and every shift in your data can be seen, understood, and acted upon.

By integrating these techniques into your data visualization practice, you not only enhance your analytical capabilities but also become a more persuasive communicator. In an era where data is abundant and time is of the essence, the ability to quickly and accurately interpret change over time is an invaluable skill.

This chapter has equipped you with a comprehensive understanding of the various methods to visualize time-based data. From the simplicity and power of line charts to the detailed nuance of fan charts, from the clear comparisons of slope charts to the impactful volume representation of area charts, and finally, to the dynamic insights offered by connected scatterplots and the organizational clarity of Gantt charts, you are now ready to tackle any time-series data challenge.

Harness the power of these visualizations to make informed decisions, share compelling stories, and drive meaningful change. With practice and attention to detail, your visualizations will not only display data—they will transform it into an engaging narrative that captivates and motivates your audience.

Let this chapter be a stepping stone to mastering the art of time-based data storytelling. Every chart you create is an opportunity to reveal insights that might otherwise remain hidden in a sea of numbers. As you apply these methods in your work, you will find that effective data visualization becomes a natural extension of your analytical thinking, making you a more insightful and impactful communicator.

With the foundation of visualizing change over time now firmly in place, you have a robust set of tools to present trends and patterns with clarity and purpose. The journey from raw data to an insightful narrative is an evolving process, and with each visualization, you learn to harness the dynamic nature of your data more effectively.

Embrace these methods, experiment with different approaches, and most importantly, let your data tell its story. The techniques covered in this chapter are designed to empower you, whether you are presenting quarterly business reviews, forecasting future trends, or managing complex projects. Your ability to visualize change over time is not only a technical skill but a critical element in effective communication and decision-making.

As you progress further into the world of data visualization, keep exploring, refining, and innovating. The tools and techniques discussed here are just the beginning of a broader journey toward becoming a masterful storyteller with data. Happy visualizing!

3.

COMPARISON & RANKING (HIGHLIGHTING DIFFERENCES & SIMILARITIES)

Comparison is one of the most common purposes of data visualization. Whether you're evaluating sales performance, ranking competitors, or analyzing market trends, effective visual comparisons can help reveal patterns, gaps, and relationships that might otherwise go unnoticed. In this chapter, we'll explore different chart types specifically designed for comparison and ranking, helping you choose the right one based on your data's complexity and purpose.

Bar Graphs: The Most Versatile Tool

Bar graphs are one of the most fundamental and widely used tools for comparing data. They are simple, effective, and easy to interpret, making them the go-to choice for many professionals.

When to Use Bar Graphs

- Comparing discrete categories (e.g., revenue by region, test scores by student).

- Displaying ranking (e.g., top-selling products).
- Showing trends over time when grouped into categories (e.g., quarterly profits by department).

Best Practices for Bar Graphs

- Use a consistent color scheme to avoid confusion.
- Arrange bars in descending order for easier ranking interpretation.
- Use horizontal bars for long category names to improve readability.
- Keep bars spaced evenly for clarity.

Stacked & Diverging Bars: Showing Proportions

Stacked and diverging bar charts build upon basic bar graphs to show proportions within a category.

Stacked Bar Charts

- Used to break down a total into subcategories.
- Ideal for visualizing distributions within a dataset.
- Example: Showing the percentage of mobile vs. desktop traffic across different months.

Diverging Bar Charts

- Best for displaying data with positive and negative values.
- Commonly used in survey results, where responses range from strongly disagree to strongly agree.
- Example: Comparing customer sentiment before and after a product launch.

Tip: Keep the number of segments reasonable (preferably under five) to maintain clarity.

Bubble Charts: Visualizing Multiple Variables

Bubble charts add another layer of information by incorporating a third variable through bubble size.

When to Use Bubble Charts

- Comparing three variables in a single chart.
- Showing relationships where size matters (e.g., population vs. income vs. GDP per capita).
- Visualizing correlations while emphasizing magnitude.

Best Practices for Bubble Charts

- Ensure bubble size is proportional and does not mislead the viewer.
- Use clear labels to avoid confusion.

- Consider color coding to categorize data points.

Waterfall Charts: Understanding Cumulative Change

Waterfall charts are perfect for showing how an initial value is affected by incremental changes, whether positive or negative.

When to Use Waterfall Charts

- Analyzing financial data (e.g., tracking revenue and expenses).
- Showing how a starting value evolves step by step.
- Demonstrating changes over time or across processes.

Best Practices for Waterfall Charts

- Use color to differentiate increases and decreases.
- Label each step clearly.
- Provide a reference line to show the initial and final values.

Sankey Diagrams: Visualizing Flow & Movement

Sankey diagrams are specialized charts used to depict flow between different entities, such as energy consumption, financial transactions, or website traffic.

When to Use Sankey Diagrams

- Showing how resources flow from one stage to another.
- Analyzing customer journeys in a funnel.
- Visualizing financial allocations.

Best Practices for Sankey Diagrams

- Keep the number of categories manageable for readability.
- Use intuitive colors to represent different flow paths.
- Ensure flow thickness is proportional to the data value.

Marimekko Charts: Showing Proportions in a Grid

Marimekko charts (also called mosaic plots) combine aspects of stacked bar charts and area charts to show proportions in a grid format.

When to Use Marimekko Charts

- Comparing market share by category and region.
- Showing relative contributions of different segments.
- Analyzing two variables in a single visualization.

Best Practices for Marimekko Charts

- Keep the number of categories limited to maintain clarity.
- Use contrasting colors for different segments.
- Ensure the chart is not overly complex for the audience.

Bullet Charts: A Smarter Alternative to Gauges

Bullet charts provide a more compact and informative alternative to traditional gauge charts, often used in performance dashboards.

When to Use Bullet Charts

- Measuring progress against a target (e.g., sales vs. goal).
- Tracking performance metrics efficiently.
- Replacing ineffective gauge charts that waste space.

Best Practices for Bullet Charts

- Use color gradients to indicate progress.
- Include clear benchmarks for reference.
- Avoid unnecessary embellishments that might distract from the data.

Dumbbell Plots: Emphasizing Differences in Data

Dumbbell plots (also known as gap charts) are excellent for highlighting differences between two points, making them useful for before-and-after comparisons.

When to Use Dumbbell Plots

- Comparing changes across two time points.

- Showing gaps or disparities in performance.
- Analyzing differences in demographics or policies.

Best Practices for Dumbbell Plots

- Use clear markers to highlight the start and end values.
- Keep axis labels concise and informative.
- Choose appropriate colors to make the differences stand out.

Conclusion

Effective comparison and ranking charts allow us to quickly analyze differences, patterns, and trends within our data. Choosing the right visualization method depends on the complexity of your data, the story you want to tell, and how much detail your audience needs. By following best practices and selecting the appropriate chart type, you can present compelling, insightful, and actionable visualizations that drive better decision-making.

In the next chapter, we'll dive into **distribution charts**, where we explore how data points are spread across a range and uncover deeper insights hidden in raw numbers.

4.

DISTRIBUTIONS & VARIABILITY (UNDERSTANDING DATA SPREAD & PATTERNS)

Data distribution is one of the most critical aspects of understanding any dataset. By visualizing how data points are spread across a range, we can uncover trends, identify anomalies, and make more informed decisions. Unlike simple comparisons, distribution charts reveal the shape of data, highlighting areas of concentration, gaps, and extreme values.

In this chapter, we'll explore several powerful visualization techniques that help analyze distributions and variability effectively. Whether you're working with finance, demographics, or experimental data, these charts will enhance your ability to interpret trends and communicate insights clearly.

Histograms: The Backbone of Distributions

Histograms are the foundation of distribution analysis. They allow us to see how data is distributed by grouping values into bins and showing their frequency.

When to Use Histograms

- Understanding the spread of a dataset.
- Identifying skewness (left-skewed, right-skewed, or normal distribution).
- Spotting clusters and gaps in the data.

Best Practices for Histograms

- Choose the right number of bins: Too few can oversimplify trends, while too many can introduce noise.
- Use consistent bin widths to avoid misleading patterns.
- Clearly label axes and provide a descriptive title.

Example:

Imagine you're analyzing customer purchase amounts. A histogram can reveal whether most purchases fall within a specific range, helping businesses adjust pricing strategies.

Dot Plots vs. Strip Plots: When to Use Each

Dot plots and strip plots serve similar purposes but work best in different scenarios.

Dot Plots

- Ideal for small datasets.
- Each dot represents a single data point.

- Good for comparing distributions across categories.

Strip Plots

- Useful for larger datasets.
- Can overlap data points, reducing clutter.
- Often combined with box plots for deeper insights.

Example:

A dot plot might work well for visualizing test scores in a small classroom, while a strip plot would be better suited for analyzing sales data across thousands of transactions.

Ridgeline Plots: Comparing Multiple Distributions

Ridgeline plots stack multiple distribution curves on top of each other, making them great for comparing trends across different groups.

When to Use Ridgeline Plots

- Analyzing trends over time (e.g., yearly temperature changes).
- Comparing distributions across categories (e.g., salaries by job title).
- Identifying shifts in data patterns.

Best Practices for Ridgeline Plots

- Use smooth density curves to improve readability.
- Maintain a balance between overlap and separation.
- Choose a clear color scheme to distinguish groups.

Example:

If you were studying the distribution of movie ratings over decades, a ridgeline plot would allow you to see how audience preferences have evolved.

Box Plots: Spotting Outliers & Trends

Box plots (or whisker plots) are a compact way to summarize data distribution, highlighting medians, quartiles, and outliers.

Key Features of a Box Plot

- **Median (Central Line):** The middle value of the dataset.
- **Interquartile Range (IQR):** The spread between the 25th and 75th percentiles.
- **Whiskers:** Show the range of non-outlier data.
- **Outliers (Dots or Asterisks):** Data points significantly outside the expected range.

When to Use Box Plots

- Comparing distributions across different categories.
- Identifying outliers in financial or experimental data.

- Summarizing large datasets quickly.

Example:

If a company wants to compare employee salaries across departments, a box plot can highlight differences and detect potential disparities.

Candlestick Charts: Financial Data Visualization

Candlestick charts are widely used in stock market analysis, providing a detailed view of price movements over time.

Key Components of a Candlestick Chart

- **Body:** Represents the opening and closing prices.
- **Wicks (Shadows):** Indicate the highest and lowest prices.
- **Colors:** Green (or white) for price increases, red (or black) for price decreases.

When to Use Candlestick Charts

- Analyzing daily, weekly, or monthly stock price trends.
- Identifying market patterns and reversal signals.
- Understanding volatility in financial markets.

Example:

A trader monitoring Tesla's stock price over a month would rely on candlestick charts to spot trends and potential buying or selling opportunities.

Violin Plots: Combining Box Plots & KDEs

Violin plots enhance traditional box plots by incorporating kernel density estimates (KDEs), which show the probability distribution of the data.

When to Use Violin Plots

- When you need both summary statistics and a detailed distribution.
- Comparing multiple distributions with different shapes.
- Highlighting multimodal distributions (multiple peaks in data).

Best Practices for Violin Plots

- Use side-by-side violin plots for category comparisons.
- Avoid over-smoothing, which can distort the data.
- Clearly label key statistical markers (e.g., median, quartiles).

Example:

If researchers want to compare test score distributions across different schools, violin plots can show both the spread and concentration of scores in one visualization.

Population Pyramids: Demographic Analysis

Population pyramids are a specialized type of bar chart used to visualize age and gender distributions.

When to Use Population Pyramids

- Analyzing demographic trends in a country or region.
- Understanding workforce composition.
- Forecasting future population changes.

Best Practices for Population Pyramids

- Use contrasting colors for male and female distributions.
- Keep age intervals consistent for accurate comparisons.
- Provide historical data alongside projections for deeper insights.

Example:

A government agency analyzing retirement trends might use a population pyramid to determine if an aging population will strain social services.

Beeswarm Plots: Enhancing Data Density

Beeswarm plots improve upon traditional scatter plots by preventing data points from overlapping, creating a more informative visualization.

When to Use Beeswarm Plots

- Displaying large amounts of individual data points.
- Highlighting clusters, gaps, and outliers.
- Providing a detailed view of data distribution.

Best Practices for Beeswarm Plots

- Use transparency to avoid visual clutter.
- Combine with box plots for added statistical insight.
- Label key categories clearly.

Example:

A scientist analyzing reaction times across different test groups might use a beeswarm plot to reveal subtle patterns that a box plot alone might miss.

Conclusion

Understanding distributions is key to making sense of complex datasets. Whether you're identifying trends, detecting anomalies, or making comparisons, the right visualization technique can transform raw numbers into actionable insights.

- **Histograms** lay the foundation for understanding distributions.
- **Dot and strip plots** provide granular detail for smaller datasets.
- **Ridgeline plots** are great for comparing multiple distributions.
- **Box and violin plots** reveal outliers and data density.
- **Candlestick charts** serve as a powerful tool for financial analysis.
- **Population pyramids** provide demographic insights.
- **Beeswarm plots** help visualize dense data effectively.

By mastering these techniques, you'll be able to extract deeper insights from your data and communicate them more effectively.

In the next chapter, we'll explore **part-to-whole visualizations**, where we analyze how individual components contribute to a larger whole.

5.

PART-TO-WHOLE RELATIONSHIPS (PROPORTIONS, SEGMENTS & COMPOSITION)

Understanding part-to-whole relationships is crucial when working with data that represents proportions, segments, or hierarchical structures. Whether analyzing market share, budget allocation, or customer demographics, choosing the right visualization can make the difference between clarity and confusion.

In this chapter, we'll explore the best ways to represent proportions and composition, helping you avoid misleading visuals and select charts that tell the most accurate and compelling story.

Pie Charts: When (and When Not) to Use Them

Pie charts are one of the most widely recognized visualizations for showing proportions, but they are also one of the most misused. While they can effectively communicate part-to-whole relationships, they often fall short when dealing with more than a few categories.

When to Use Pie Charts

When displaying **a small number of categories** (ideally 2–5).
When the data **adds up to 100%** and represents a **single moment in time**.
When you want to **quickly compare a dominant category** to others.

When to Avoid Pie Charts

When you have **too many categories**—this makes slices too small and difficult to distinguish.
When you need to make **precise comparisons**—bar charts are better for this.
When comparing multiple datasets—pie charts don't scale well side by side.

Best Practices for Pie Charts

- **Limit the number of slices** to improve readability.
- **Use clear labels** instead of relying solely on a legend.
- **Sort slices logically**, placing the largest segment first and moving clockwise.
- **Use contrasting colors** for differentiation but avoid overly bright or distracting color schemes.

Example:

A company analyzing revenue sources might use a pie chart to show that 60% of income comes from product sales, 30% from services, and 10% from licensing.

However, if they need to compare revenue sources across multiple years, a **stacked bar chart** would be a better alternative.

Tree Maps: A Better Alternative to Pie Charts

A **tree map** is a powerful visualization that uses nested rectangles to represent hierarchical data. Each rectangle's size corresponds to its proportion within the whole, making it an excellent choice when dealing with multiple categories and subcategories.

When to Use Tree Maps

When comparing **many categories at once**—more effective than a cluttered pie chart.
When visualizing **hierarchical structures** (e.g., company departments, website traffic sources).
When displaying **relative proportions clearly** without relying on shape perception.

Best Practices for Tree Maps

- **Use intuitive grouping** to structure data logically.
- **Maintain a good aspect ratio**—avoid long, narrow rectangles.
- **Use shading or color gradients** to show variations within a category.
- **Keep labels readable** by ensuring rectangles aren't too small.

Example:

An e-commerce company analyzing sales by category could use a tree map to show that electronics take up 40% of total sales, clothing 30%, and smaller rectangles for niche products like books, accessories, and toys.

Compared to a pie chart, a tree map **allows for deeper granularity**, making it easier to compare multiple segments at a glance.

Sunburst Charts: Visualizing Hierarchical Proportions

A **sunburst chart** is an advanced version of a pie chart that displays hierarchical data in concentric rings. Each level of the hierarchy is represented by a new ring, making it useful for showing how subcategories contribute to a whole.

When to Use Sunburst Charts

When visualizing **multi-level hierarchical data** (e.g., organizational structures, website navigation).

When you need to show **how categories break down into subcategories**.

When illustrating **complex relationships** that would be difficult to interpret in a simple pie chart.

Best Practices for Sunburst Charts

- **Keep inner circles simple**, focusing on major categories.
- **Use clear color distinctions** to separate levels effectively.
- **Ensure segment proportions accurately reflect data values** to avoid distortion.
- **Consider interactive sunbursts** in digital formats to allow for drill-down exploration.

Example:

A university analyzing its student population by faculty and major could use a sunburst chart. The **innermost ring**represents the university's total enrollment, the **second ring** represents major faculties (e.g., Science, Arts, Business), and the **outer rings** break down into individual majors (e.g., Biology, Literature, Marketing).

Compared to a tree map, a sunburst chart provides a **more visually engaging and circular representation** of hierarchy while still preserving the part-to-whole structure.

Nightingale Rose Charts: Circular Comparisons

A **Nightingale Rose Chart**, also known as a polar area diagram, is a variation of a pie chart that uses wedges to show magnitudes, rather than just proportions. It was first developed by Florence Nightingale to illustrate the causes of death in military hospitals, making data-driven decision-making more effective.

Unlike a standard pie chart where the angle of each slice represents a percentage, in a Nightingale chart, **the angle remains equal, but the radius changes** based on data values. This makes it easier to compare magnitudes visually.

When to Use Nightingale Rose Charts

When comparing **seasonal trends** or cyclic data (e.g., monthly sales, weather patterns).

When displaying **data where values are naturally radial**, such as directions or time-based statistics.

When highlighting **variations in magnitude rather than strict proportions**.

Best Practices for Nightingale Rose Charts

- **Ensure clear labeling** of different sections to improve readability.
- **Avoid excessive segments**, which can make it difficult to interpret patterns.
- **Use a meaningful order** (e.g., chronological for time-based data).
- **Be cautious with small values**, as they may be harder to distinguish in circular format.

Example:

A retail store analyzing sales by month might use a Nightingale rose chart to show peak shopping periods, with larger radii indicating higher sales months (e.g., November and December due to holiday shopping).

Compared to a bar chart, a Nightingale rose chart **offers a more visually engaging way to spot cyclical trends** while still maintaining the part-to-whole relationship.

Conclusion: Choosing the Right Chart for Part-to-Whole Data

Understanding part-to-whole relationships is essential for anyone working with data, whether in business, healthcare, finance, or education. Selecting the right chart depends on the complexity of the data and the message you want to convey.

- **Pie charts** work well for small datasets but become ineffective with too many categories.
- **Tree maps** are an excellent alternative for handling **larger datasets and hierarchical structures**.
- **Sunburst charts** build upon tree maps by providing **a radial visualization of hierarchical data**.
- **Nightingale rose charts** offer a **unique way to compare magnitudes** in a circular format, making them great for cyclic trends.

When deciding on a visualization, always consider:

Clarity – Does the audience instantly grasp the key insights?

Accuracy – Does the chart avoid distortions and misleading representations?

Efficiency – Can the message be conveyed quickly without unnecessary complexity?

By mastering these visualization techniques, you'll be able to **transform raw numbers into clear, compelling stories**that help decision-makers take action.

What's Next?

Now that we've covered part-to-whole relationships, it's time to dive into **relationship charts**, where we analyze connections, correlations, and dependencies between variables.

6.

RELATIONSHIPS & CORRELATIONS (FINDING PATTERNS & CONNECTIONS IN DATA)

Understanding how variables relate to each other is at the heart of data analysis. Whether uncovering hidden trends, spotting anomalies, or mapping out complex interactions, visualizing relationships helps transform raw data into meaningful insights.

In this chapter, we will explore the best ways to analyze **correlations, dependencies, and connections** between different variables. From simple scatter plots to advanced network diagrams, we will break down each visualization method and when to use it.

Scatter Plots: Spotting Trends and Outliers

A **scatter plot** is one of the most fundamental ways to visualize relationships between two numerical variables. Each point on the graph represents a single data observation, with its x-coordinate and y-coordinate corresponding to the values of two variables.

When to Use Scatter Plots

- When analyzing the relationship between two continuous variables, such as height versus weight or income versus education level.

- When detecting trends, such as positive or negative correlations.

- When identifying outliers—points that do not follow the general trend.

Key Patterns in Scatter Plots

- **Positive correlation**: As one variable increases, the other tends to increase.

- **Negative correlation**: As one variable increases, the other decreases.

- **No correlation**: No clear relationship exists between the variables.

- **Clusters**: Groups of data points that form distinct patterns.

- **Outliers**: Data points that deviate significantly from the general trend.

Scatter plots are widely used in finance, health sciences, and social research to analyze relationships between variables.

Radar Charts: Comparing Multidimensional Data

Radar charts, also called **spider charts**, are used to compare multiple variables across different categories. They plot data points on axes that radiate from a central point, connecting them to form a web-like shape.

When to Use Radar Charts

- When comparing **multiple categories** across several quantitative variables.

- When analyzing **performance metrics**, such as comparing the skills of different employees or the specifications of competing products.

- When visualizing **strengths and weaknesses** in various aspects of data.

Strengths and Limitations of Radar Charts

Radar charts are useful when you want to show patterns across multiple dimensions. However, they can become cluttered and difficult to read when too many variables are included. In such cases, alternative visualizations like bar charts or parallel coordinate plots might be more effective.

Chord Diagrams: Showing Complex Relationships

A **chord diagram** is a circular visualization that represents relationships between different categories. It is particularly useful for illustrating **flows, interactions, and interdependencies** among multiple entities.

When to Use Chord Diagrams

- When analyzing **relationships between multiple categories**, such as trade relationships between countries.

- When visualizing **network connections**, such as shared users across different platforms.

- When showing **movement or flow of resources** between different groups.

How to Read a Chord Diagram

Chord diagrams consist of arcs along the perimeter of a circle, each representing a category. Lines or "chords" connect these arcs, showing the strength and direction of relationships. The thicker the line, the stronger the connection.

While chord diagrams are visually striking, they should be used carefully, as they can be overwhelming if too many connections are displayed at once.

Network Diagrams: Mapping Connections

Network diagrams, also known as **graph visualizations**, depict relationships between entities using **nodes and edges**. Each node represents an entity, and the edges represent the relationships between them.

When to Use Network Diagrams

- When analyzing **social networks**, such as interactions between people on social media.

- When mapping **connections in complex systems**, such as supply chain relationships or biological pathways.

- When visualizing **hierarchical structures**, such as organizational charts.

Key Features of Network Diagrams

- **Central nodes**: Entities with many connections, often acting as influencers or key hubs.

- **Clusters**: Groups of nodes that are more connected to each other than to the rest of the network.

- **Directed vs. undirected edges**: Some relationships have direction (e.g., one person following another on social media), while others are mutual (e.g., friends in a network).

Network diagrams are commonly used in cybersecurity, epidemiology, and business intelligence to understand relationships between different components of a system.

Tree Diagrams: Hierarchies and Structures

Tree diagrams are used to **represent hierarchical relationships** in data. They start from a root node and branch out into subcategories, making them useful for understanding structures and dependencies.

When to Use Tree Diagrams

- When displaying **organizational structures**, such as company hierarchies.

- When analyzing **decision trees**, such as in machine learning models.

- When visualizing **classification systems**, such as biological taxonomies or website navigation.

Tree diagrams are excellent for breaking down complex information into simpler, more digestible parts. However, they can become large and difficult to read if too many levels are included.

Parallel Coordinates Plots: Exploring Multivariate Data

A **parallel coordinates plot** is used for visualizing **multivariate data**, where each variable is represented as a vertical axis. Data points are connected across these axes, forming lines that show patterns and trends.

When to Use Parallel Coordinates Plots

- When analyzing **high-dimensional data**, such as comparing financial portfolios or customer preferences.

- When identifying **trends and anomalies** across multiple factors.

- When exploring **correlations between different variables** in complex datasets.

Parallel coordinates plots can reveal relationships that might be missed in other types of visualizations. However, they can become cluttered if too many data points are included, making filtering and interaction essential for clarity.

Conclusion

Visualizing relationships and correlations in data is essential for identifying patterns, trends, and connections that might not be obvious at first glance. From **scatter plots** that highlight trends to **network diagrams** that map out complex interactions, choosing the right visualization depends on the type of relationships you need to explore.

By mastering these techniques, you can uncover hidden insights in your data, improve decision-making, and communicate your findings effectively. In the next chapter, we will dive into **geographical visualizations**, exploring maps and spatial data techniques to bring location-based insights to life.

7.

GEOGRAPHICAL DATA VISUALIZATION (MAPPING DATA EFFECTIVELY)

Mapping data is one of the most powerful ways to understand spatial patterns, relationships, and trends. Whether tracking population distribution, visualizing traffic flow, or analyzing regional sales performance, **geographical data visualization** helps make complex spatial data more intuitive.

In this chapter, we will explore different mapping techniques, their strengths and weaknesses, and when to use them for maximum impact.

Choropleth Maps: Color-Coded Geographic Data

A **choropleth map** is one of the most widely used geographic data visualizations. It represents values across geographic regions using **shades of color**, making it easy to compare areas at a glance.

When to Use Choropleth Maps

- When showing **density or intensity** of a variable, such as population, income levels, or election results.

- When analyzing **regional patterns and trends**, like unemployment rates across states or countries.

- When comparing **normalized data**, such as percentages rather than raw numbers.

Best Practices for Choropleth Maps

- **Use an appropriate color scale**: Sequential color schemes work best for continuous data (e.g., temperature), while diverging color scales highlight differences around a central value (e.g., profit vs. loss).

- **Avoid using too many colors**: Too many variations can confuse the reader. Stick to a clear gradient.

- **Normalize data properly**: Display percentages or per capita values instead of absolute counts to avoid misleading conclusions.

Choropleth maps are commonly used in demographics, economics, and political analysis. However, they can sometimes obscure data variations within regions, which is where other mapping techniques can be useful.

Proportional Symbol Maps: Scaling Data on Maps

A **proportional symbol map** uses differently sized circles, squares, or other markers to represent varying magnitudes of data at specific locations. Unlike choropleth maps, which color entire regions, proportional symbol maps focus on individual data points.

When to Use Proportional Symbol Maps

- When visualizing **absolute values** at specific locations, such as city populations or sales figures per store.

- When comparing data **within a region** without relying on color gradients.

- When showing **relative differences** between multiple locations.

Best Practices for Proportional Symbol Maps

- **Use clear scaling**: Ensure that symbol sizes accurately represent data values.

- **Minimize overlap**: Too many large symbols in close proximity can make interpretation difficult.

- **Combine with choropleth maps**: Sometimes, layering proportional symbols over a choropleth map enhances clarity.

Proportional symbol maps are particularly effective in business analytics, urban planning, and public health studies, where **localized** insights matter.

Flow Maps: Tracking Movements & Trends

Flow maps are used to visualize **movement between locations**, such as migration patterns, trade routes, or traffic flows. They display directional lines or arrows that indicate the path and volume of movement.

When to Use Flow Maps

- When tracking **people, goods, or information** moving from one place to another.

- When illustrating **supply chain logistics** or global trade.

- When analyzing **commuting patterns** or flight routes.

Key Features of Flow Maps

- **Directional arrows**: Indicate the origin and destination of movement.

- **Line thickness**: Represents the magnitude of movement—thicker lines indicate higher volume.

- **Color coding**: Can differentiate between categories, such as inbound vs. outbound flows.

Flow maps are widely used in **transportation planning, economic geography, and logistics management** to optimize movement efficiency.

Radial Flow Maps: Circular Flow Representation

A **radial flow map** is a special type of flow map that displays movements or connections originating from a central point, extending outward in a radial pattern.

When to Use Radial Flow Maps

- When mapping **air traffic routes** from a central hub.

- When visualizing **distribution networks**, such as shipments from a warehouse.

- When showing **communication patterns**, such as internet traffic across different regions.

Best Practices for Radial Flow Maps

- **Keep labels clear**: Too many overlapping lines can make the visualization cluttered.

- **Use interactive tools**: Radial flow maps are often more effective when interactive, allowing users to hover over specific flows for more details.

- **Limit the number of connections**: Too many radial flows can reduce readability—focus on key trends.

Radial flow maps are commonly used in **logistics, air travel, and network communication analysis**, where understanding **centralized** movement is critical.

Network Flow Maps: Mapping Connections & Traffic

A **network flow map** is used to show **connections between multiple locations**, often forming a web-like structure. Unlike radial flow maps, which emphasize a central hub, network flow maps display **complex interactions** between multiple points.

When to Use Network Flow Maps

- When visualizing **communication networks**, such as phone call volumes between different cities.

- When analyzing **supply chain networks** involving multiple suppliers and distributors.

- When tracking **global internet traffic** or **electric grid connections**.

Best Practices for Network Flow Maps

- **Minimize clutter**: Too many connections can make the map unreadable, so consider filtering for clarity.

- **Differentiate link strengths**: Use varying line thickness or opacity to indicate the strength of each connection.

- **Use clustering techniques**: If possible, group related nodes together to make patterns more obvious.

Network flow maps are valuable in **telecommunications, trade networks, and infrastructure planning**, where **interconnectivity** matters more than linear movement.

Distributive Flow Maps: Geographic Spread & Density

A **distributive flow map** represents how something spreads across a geographic area, whether it be **disease outbreaks, resource allocation, or internet access**. Unlike standard flow maps that focus on direct movement, distributive flow maps emphasize the **diffusion** of data across space.

When to Use Distributive Flow Maps

- When mapping **epidemic outbreaks**, such as the spread of a virus over time.

- When analyzing **resource distribution**, such as emergency aid reaching affected areas.

- When tracking **market penetration**, such as product adoption across different regions.

Best Practices for Distributive Flow Maps

- **Use gradual color transitions**: Since data spreads out rather than flowing directly, smooth gradients often work better than hard boundaries.

- **Overlay with other data layers**: For example, combining a distributive flow map with population density can provide additional insights.

- **Animate for time-series data**: If possible, showing distribution over time enhances clarity.

Distributive flow maps are widely used in **public health, environmental science, and market research**, where understanding **how things spread** is crucial.

Conclusion

Geographical data visualization is a **critical tool** for analyzing location-based insights. Whether you need to track migration patterns, analyze business markets, or visualize global trade flows, **choosing the right map type** makes all the difference.

- **Choropleth maps** provide a **color-coded** representation of data intensity.

- **Proportional symbol maps** scale **data points** for better comparison.

- **Flow maps** track **movement trends** over space.

- **Radial flow maps** highlight **centralized** connections.

- **Network flow maps** reveal **complex web-like relationships.**

- **Distributive flow maps** illustrate **geographic spread** of data over time.

By mastering these mapping techniques, you can transform raw geographic data into **clear, actionable insights** that drive better decision-making.

In the next chapter, we will explore **tables, pictograms, and infographic design**—key elements for presenting data **beyond traditional charts and graphs.**

8.

TABLES, PICTOGRAMS & INFOGRAPHICS
(MAKING DATA VISUALLY ENGAGING)

Visualizing data isn't just about charts and maps. Sometimes, the most effective way to communicate complex information is through **tables, pictograms, or infographics**. These tools allow you to present data in a way that is both **structured and visually appealing**, making it easier for your audience to **digest, compare, and remember key insights**.

In this chapter, we'll explore when to use tables instead of charts, how to design **clear and effective tables**, the power of **pictograms** for simplifying complex data, and how to craft **engaging infographics** that tell a compelling story.

When to Use Tables Instead of Charts

Charts and graphs are great for revealing **trends, relationships, and patterns**, but sometimes, a simple **table** is the best choice.

When Should You Use Tables?

- **Exact numerical values matter**: If your audience needs to see specific numbers rather than general trends, tables provide more precision.

- **Comparing multiple variables at once**: When you need to display **multiple categories, dates, or regions**, tables allow for side-by-side comparisons.

- **Data is too detailed for a chart**: If there are too many data points, a chart can become cluttered, while a table remains clear and readable.

- **No clear trend exists**: When numbers don't follow a pattern (e.g., random survey results), a chart may not provide meaningful insights, but a table can list the values logically.

When Should You Avoid Tables?

- When you want to emphasize **trends over time** (use a line chart instead).

- When you need to highlight **proportions** (a pie chart or bar chart may work better).

- When data is **too dense**—if a table has **too many rows and columns**, it can overwhelm the reader.

A well-designed table helps **organize data efficiently**, making it easy to scan and extract information quickly.

Designing Readable & Effective Tables

A good table is **clear, concise, and visually structured**. Follow these best practices to enhance readability:

1. Keep It Simple

- Avoid unnecessary lines, borders, and colors.

- Focus on **essential data** and remove clutter.

2. Use Alignment Strategically

- **Left-align text** (easier to read).

- **Right-align numbers** (makes comparing values easier).

- **Center-align headers** for a clean look.

3. Highlight Key Data

- Use **bold text** or background shading for important figures.

- Sort data in a **logical order** (e.g., highest to lowest).

- If the table is large, use **row shading** to improve readability.

4. Provide Context

- Add **row and column headers** to explain what the data represents.

- Include **units** (%, $, kg, etc.) so numbers are easily understood.

Pictograms: Simplifying Complex Data

A **pictogram** (or pictograph) uses **icons or images** to represent data, making information more engaging and **easy to interpret at a glance**.

Why Use Pictograms?

- **Simplifies complex data**: Instead of overwhelming readers with numbers, pictograms present data in a more relatable way.

- **Enhances memorability**: People remember visuals better than raw numbers.

- **Engages audiences**: Especially useful in presentations, social media, and reports where engagement matters.

Examples of Pictograms in Action

- **Population growth**: Instead of writing "1 in 5 people," show five stick figures, with one shaded in.

- **Energy consumption**: Display icons of light bulbs to represent different levels of usage.

- **Product sales**: Use shopping cart icons, where each icon represents a certain number of sales.

Best Practices for Pictograms

- **Keep icons simple**: Overly detailed images can distract from the data.

- **Use consistent sizing**: Each icon should represent the same value (e.g., 1 icon = 10,000 units).

- **Limit colors**: Stick to a few contrasting shades to maintain clarity.

Pictograms are commonly used in **infographics, educational materials, and business reports** to make **data more relatable** and **visually appealing**.

Creating Engaging Infographics

Infographics **combine data, visuals, and storytelling** into one **compelling visual** that is easy to understand. Unlike static charts, infographics **guide the viewer** through key takeaways, making them **highly shareable and engaging**.

What Makes a Great Infographic?

1. **A Clear Message**

   o Start with a central theme—what story are you telling?

   o Avoid cramming too much information; **focus on key insights**.

2. **Visually Appealing Layout**

   o Use **sections** to break down content logically.

   o Mix **icons, charts, and short text** for variety.

3. **Consistent Color Scheme**

   o Stick to a **limited color palette** that enhances readability.

   o Use **contrasting colors** to highlight important points.

4. **Readable Fonts**

- o Use **bold headers** and **short, scannable text**.

- o Avoid decorative fonts—stick to clean, professional typography.

Types of Infographics

- **Statistical Infographics**: Uses charts and numbers to present data-heavy topics.

- **Process Infographics**: Breaks down a step-by-step process visually.

- **Comparison Infographics**: Highlights differences between two concepts (e.g., benefits of two different products).

- **Timeline Infographics**: Showcases historical trends or projections into the future.

Infographics are widely used in **marketing, journalism, and education** because they turn **boring statistics into engaging, easy-to-understand content**.

Conclusion

Tables, pictograms, and infographics are **powerful alternatives** to traditional charts. Knowing **when and how to use them** can significantly enhance how you present data.

- **Tables** work best when **exact numbers matter** and multiple variables need to be compared.

- **Pictograms** simplify **complex data** using icons, making numbers more relatable.

- **Infographics** blend **data, visuals, and storytelling** into engaging, memorable formats.

By mastering these techniques, you'll be able to **communicate data more effectively**, **engage your audience**, and create **compelling visual narratives** that capture attention.

9.

PRINCIPLES OF EFFECTIVE DESIGN (OPTIMIZING CHARTS FOR MAXIMUM IMPACT)

Creating an effective chart is not just about plotting data—it is about **communicating information clearly and persuasively**. Poorly designed visuals can mislead, confuse, or overwhelm an audience, while well-optimized visualizations can highlight key insights, enhance comprehension, and support better decision-making.

This chapter will cover **seven essential principles of effective design**, how to **optimize chart elements** for clarity, and the importance of **color selection, contrast, and white space**. By following these guidelines, you can ensure your charts are **both visually appealing and highly functional**.

7 Essential Principles for Stunning Visuals

There are seven key design principles that every great data visualization follows. Whether designing a simple bar graph or a complex interactive dashboard, these principles will ensure **clarity, engagement, and accuracy**.

1. Keep It Simple

Simplicity is the foundation of effective design. **Less is more** when it comes to data visualization. Unnecessary elements that do not contribute to understanding should be removed.

- **Do:** Use clear labels, straightforward designs, and focus only on relevant data.

- **Do Not:** Overload your chart with excessive colors, 3D effects, or decorative elements that add clutter.

2. Ensure Readability

A chart is ineffective if the audience struggles to read it. **Text should be legible, labels should be clear, and data points should not be crowded.**

- **Do:** Use readable fonts, proper spacing, and ensure that all labels are visible.

- **Do Not:** Shrink text too much or overload the chart with excessive annotations.

3. Use the Right Chart for the Right Data

One of the biggest mistakes in data visualization is using the **wrong chart type** for the dataset. For example, a pie chart may seem like a good option for showing proportions, but if there are too many categories, a bar chart would be **far clearer**.

- **Do:** Match the chart type to the insight being highlighted.

- **Do Not:** Use a chart just because it "looks interesting" if it does not accurately represent the data.

4. Prioritize Data Accuracy

Misleading visualizations can **distort reality** and misinform the audience. Avoid **manipulating scales, truncating axes, or using perspective distortions** that alter the perception of the data.

- **Do:** Use uniform scales and maintain the integrity of the data.

- **Do Not:** Cut off axes or exaggerate trends with misleading visual effects.

5. Highlight Key Insights

A well-designed chart directs attention to the most **important takeaways**. **Visual hierarchy** can be created using **color, size, contrast, and annotations** to emphasize critical points.

- **Do:** Use bold colors or callouts to highlight significant data points.

- **Do Not:** Use too many competing colors or effects that make everything stand out equally.

6. Use Consistent Design Elements

Consistency ensures that multiple charts within a report, presentation, or dashboard feel **cohesive and professional**.

- **Do:** Use the same font styles, color schemes, and chart types for similar data across different visuals.

- **Do Not:** Mix different design styles that do not align with each other.

7. Test with Real Users

The best way to determine if a visualization is effective is to **test it with the intended audience**. Different people interpret data differently, so usability testing is key.

- **Do:** Share the visualization with others and gather feedback.

- **Do Not:** Assume that just because the chart makes sense to the creator, it will be clear to everyone.

Optimizing Chart Elements for Clarity and Readability

Each element in a chart serves a purpose. **Every choice should enhance, not distract from, the message.** Below are ways to optimize key components of a visualization.

Titles and Labels

- Use **clear, descriptive titles** that immediately communicate the chart's purpose.

- Axis labels should be **concise yet informative**, avoiding unnecessary abbreviations or jargon.

- Data labels should only be used where necessary to prevent visual clutter.

Gridlines and Borders

- Keep **gridlines subtle** to avoid overpowering the data.

- Avoid using thick borders or excessive shading that can make a chart look cluttered.

Legend Placement

- Place the legend **close to the data** it describes, reducing the need for excessive eye movement.

- If a chart only contains a few categories, consider **labeling data directly** instead of using a separate legend.

Chart Scale and Axes

- Ensure **axes start at zero** when displaying bar charts to prevent misleading interpretations.

- Avoid **skewing the y-axis** in a way that exaggerates differences in data.

- Use consistent intervals on axes to ensure **accurate comparisons**.

Choosing the Right Colors and Avoiding Misuse

Color plays a **crucial role** in data visualization. It helps **differentiate categories, highlight key points, and create visual impact**. However, **misusing color** can lead to confusion and reduce readability.

Best Practices for Using Color

- Use **consistent colors** for similar data points.

- **Limit the color palette** to 4-6 distinct colors in a single visualization.

- Choose **contrasting colors** for comparisons, but avoid overly bright or clashing combinations.

- Use **neutral or muted colors** for background elements to keep focus on the data.

Common Color Mistakes to Avoid

- Using **too many colors**, making the chart look overwhelming.

- Relying on **only color** to distinguish elements, which can be inaccessible to color-blind viewers.

- Using **red-green combinations**, as they can be difficult to distinguish for those with color vision deficiencies.

- Picking **random colors** without a logical meaning or grouping.

Using Color to Emphasize Data

- Use **a single highlight color** to draw attention to a key data point.

- **Fade less relevant data** into the background to create a sense of visual hierarchy.

- Use **color gradients** to show intensity, such as temperature maps or population densities.

Using Color Palettes for Different Chart Types

Different visualization types require different **color strategies** to be effective.

- **Comparison charts (bar, column, line)** – Use a **single color family** with varying shades.

- **Proportional charts (pie, treemap, sunburst)** – Use **distinct colors** for each category, but keep them within a cohesive palette.

- **Sequential data (heatmaps, choropleth maps, density plots)** – Use **gradient scales** from light to dark to show intensity.

- **Diverging data (sentiment analysis, performance scales)** – Use **opposing color spectrums**, such as blue-to-red for negative-to-positive trends.

The Power of White Space and Minimalism

White space, or **negative space**, refers to the areas of a chart that are **left empty on purpose**. It plays a crucial role in **enhancing readability and drawing attention to the most important elements**.

Why White Space Matters

- Reduces **visual clutter**, making data easier to process.

- Helps create **clear separation** between different sections.

- Directs the viewer's **focus to key insights** without distractions.

How to Effectively Use White Space

- Avoid **cramming too many elements** into a single chart.

- Increase **margins and padding** around key areas to create breathing room.

- Use **consistent spacing** between data points, labels, and legends to maintain readability.

Final Thoughts

The most effective data visualizations are **not just visually attractive**—they are designed with **clarity, accuracy, and storytelling in mind**. By following these principles, you can **transform raw data into compelling insights** that engage and inform your audience.

By keeping your designs simple, readable, and purposeful, while optimizing color, spacing, and layout, you can ensure that **your visualizations stand out as professional, insightful, and impactful.**

10.

CHART REDESIGNS & CASE STUDIES (FIXING COMMON VISUALIZATION MISTAKES)

Creating a chart is easy, but creating an effective, clear, and impactful visualization requires skill and thoughtful design. Many charts fail to communicate insights properly due to overcomplication, poor design choices, or misleading representations. In this chapter, we will explore before-and-after redesigns, discuss common pitfalls, and analyze real-world case studies to understand what separates bad visualizations from great ones.

Before & After: Improving Common Charts

Redesigning poorly structured charts is one of the best ways to understand what makes an effective visualization. Below are some common mistakes and how they can be fixed.

Overloaded Pie Charts vs. Simplified Alternatives

Before: A Cluttered Pie Chart

Many people use pie charts to show proportions, but when too many categories are involved, they become unreadable.

Problems:

- Too many slices make it hard to compare proportions.

- Similar colors make differentiation difficult.

- Labels overlap, creating clutter.

After: A Bar Chart or Tree Map

A bar chart or tree map is a better choice for handling multiple categories.

Improvements:

- Better readability by arranging data in a logical order.

- Easier comparisons, as values can be directly compared without relying on angles.

- Minimal clutter with well-spaced, legible labels.

Misleading Bar Charts vs. Corrected Scale & Axis

Before: A Truncated Bar Chart

Some bar charts manipulate the y-axis to exaggerate differences between categories.

Problems:

- Y-axis does not start at zero, making small differences appear much larger.

- Bars are too narrow, creating a visual distortion of the data.

- The spacing between bars is inconsistent.

After: A Properly Scaled Bar Chart

Fixing the scale ensures accurate representation of data.

Improvements:

- Y-axis starts at zero to provide a true comparison.

- Bars have equal width and spacing for consistency.

- Clear labels make it easy to interpret.

Overcomplicated Line Graphs vs. Streamlined Storytelling

Before: A Cluttered Multi-Line Chart

A line chart tracking multiple data series can easily become unreadable if too many lines are included.

Problems:

- Too many lines overlap, making it difficult to track trends.

- The legend has too many entries, reducing clarity.

- Colors are too similar, causing confusion.

After: A Selective Line Chart with Annotations

Reducing unnecessary elements improves clarity.

Improvements:

- Only the most important data series are shown.

- Labels are placed directly on lines instead of using a separate legend.

- Key trends are highlighted with annotations instead of extra lines.

Simplifying Overcomplicated Visuals

Many charts include unnecessary elements that add complexity without improving comprehension. Below are common simplifications that improve clarity.

Removing Unnecessary Gridlines and Borders

Excessive gridlines and thick borders distract from the actual data. Lightening or removing them creates a cleaner presentation.

Using Direct Labeling Instead of a Legend

If a chart has only a few data series, placing labels directly on the chart eliminates the need for a separate legend.

Avoiding 3D Charts for Better Readability

Three-dimensional effects can distort data, making it harder to interpret. Using flat, two-dimensional charts enhances clarity.

Enhancing Storytelling Through Redesign

Good data visualization is not just about displaying numbers; it tells a compelling story. The following improvements enhance storytelling.

Highlighting Key Insights with Annotations

Instead of expecting the reader to find patterns on their own, annotations can direct attention to important insights.

Using Color Strategically

Applying a consistent and meaningful color scheme can help reinforce key messages. For example, using a single highlight color for the most important data point draws attention to it.

Ensuring Logical Flow in Dashboard Layouts

For dashboards, placing charts in a logical order ensures a smoother data interpretation experience. Start with an overview, then move to detailed breakdowns.

Real-World Examples of Great Data Visualization

Case Study 1: The COVID-19 Data Dashboards

Early in the pandemic, many COVID-19 dashboards provided clear, well-structured visualizations. The best ones used:

- Simple line charts to track case trends.

- Clear comparisons between different time periods.

- Effective use of color to distinguish positive and negative trends.

Case Study 2: The New York Times Electoral Maps

The New York Times uses interactive electoral maps that allow users to explore voting trends with different filters. They stand out because they:

- Use clear color schemes for different political parties.

- Provide historical comparisons for better context.

- Offer an intuitive and engaging user experience.

Final Thoughts

A well-designed visualization simplifies data, enhances comprehension, and tells a compelling story. By applying the principles in this chapter, you can improve your own charts and avoid the most common pitfalls in data visualization. Always aim for clarity, remove distractions, and highlight key insights to make your data as impactful as possible.

11.

TOOLS & RESOURCES FOR DATA VISUALIZATION *(BRINGING YOUR CHARTS TO LIFE)*

Top Free & Paid Data Visualization Tools

The journey from raw data to compelling visualizations is largely influenced by the tools you choose. These tools transform complex data sets into clear, actionable insights, and whether you're a beginner or a seasoned expert, the right tool can elevate your work. There's a variety of options available in both free and paid categories. Here's a breakdown:

Free Tools

1. **Google Data Studio**:
   Google Data Studio is one of the most popular free tools available for creating interactive reports and dashboards. It's web-based and integrates seamlessly with Google Analytics, Google Sheets, and other Google services. It offers drag-and-drop functionality, customizable themes, and collaborative features, making it an excellent choice for team-based projects.

2. **Tableau Public**:

   Tableau Public is the free version of the renowned Tableau software. It allows you to create sophisticated visualizations and share them publicly on the web. While the paid version offers additional features, the free version still provides access to many of Tableau's robust capabilities, making it a popular choice for aspiring data analysts and visualization experts.

3. **RAWGraphs**:

   RAWGraphs is an open-source data visualization framework that focuses on simplicity and ease of use. It supports a wide range of visualization types and is ideal for users looking to create visualizations quickly without steep learning curves. Its open-source nature allows for customization if needed.

4. **Power BI Desktop**:

   Power BI offers a free version of its powerful data visualization software, perfect for individuals or small teams. It enables users to create reports and dashboards, connect to various data sources, and utilize powerful features like AI-powered visual insights.

5. **Plotly**:

   Plotly provides a set of tools for creating interactive

charts and dashboards. The free version allows users to create high-quality graphs that can be embedded in web pages. Plotly's open-source library, Plotly.js, is a great option for programmers looking to build custom, interactive visualizations.

Paid Tools

1. **Tableau**:
   Tableau is the industry standard in data visualization. With its intuitive drag-and-drop interface, powerful analytics capabilities, and vast range of visualizations, it is a go-to tool for data professionals. The paid version offers advanced features like data blending, advanced mapping, and predictive analytics, making it ideal for more complex needs.

2. **Microsoft Power BI Pro**:
   While the free version of Power BI is great for individual users, the paid Pro version offers features like collaborative sharing, larger data capacity, and cloud-based reports. It integrates seamlessly with Microsoft Office tools, making it an excellent choice for those already within the Microsoft ecosystem.

3. **Qlik Sense**:

   Qlik Sense is a robust platform for creating dynamic dashboards and data visualizations. Its associative model allows users to make connections between different data sets, providing deep insights. The enterprise version offers advanced security, governance, and reporting capabilities.

4. **Sisense**:

   Sisense allows users to create interactive visualizations, but it also specializes in embedding analytics within other applications. It's an excellent tool for businesses that want to provide data-driven insights to customers or employees through custom applications.

5. **TIBCO Spotfire**:

   Spotfire is an enterprise-level tool for data analytics and visualization. It allows for the integration of predictive analytics and real-time data streams. The software is geared toward organizations that need advanced analytics capabilities, but it's intuitive enough for beginners to use effectively.

Best Software for Beginners vs. Experts

When choosing a data visualization tool, consider your experience level, the complexity of the data, and the visualizations you need. Here's a comparison of the best tools for beginners and experts:

Best Tools for Beginners

1. **Google Data Studio**:
   Google Data Studio is an excellent starting point for beginners because it's web-based, easy to use, and integrates with other Google products. It's perfect for users who are familiar with Google Sheets or Google Analytics and want to create simple but professional-looking reports and dashboards.

2. **RAWGraphs**:
   RAWGraphs is user-friendly and ideal for beginners who want to explore creative data visualizations without a steep learning curve. Its drag-and-drop interface and ready-made templates make it easy to use for quick projects.

3. **Power BI Desktop**:
   The free version of Power BI is a great entry point for those new to data visualization. The platform provides an extensive library of tutorials and online communities,

making it easier for beginners to learn the ropes while still using powerful tools.

4. **Chart.js**:

   Chart.js is a JavaScript library for creating simple charts. It's easy to implement and ideal for those who are just beginning to explore coding for data visualization. It supports bar charts, pie charts, line charts, and more.

5. **Canva**:

   While not traditionally a data visualization tool, Canva is perfect for beginners who need to create quick, aesthetically pleasing visuals. Canva's ease of use and range of templates allow non-designers to create polished infographics and charts.

Best Tools for Experts

1. **Tableau**:

   Tableau is the tool of choice for experts who need to work with large datasets, perform complex data transformations, and build interactive, dynamic dashboards. With its advanced analytics capabilities, experts can integrate predictive analytics, geospatial data, and statistical models.

2. **Qlik Sense**:

   Qlik Sense is highly regarded among experts for its in-depth analytical capabilities and associative data model. It's a tool designed for power users who want to delve deeper into data exploration and uncover insights that are not immediately obvious.

3. **D3.js**:

   D3.js is a powerful JavaScript library that allows experts to create custom, interactive data visualizations on the web. It requires a solid understanding of web development, but it offers maximum flexibility and control over the final output.

4. **Sisense**:

   Sisense offers a full suite of enterprise-grade data visualization tools, with an emphasis on integrating data from disparate sources. It's best suited for organizations looking for a data visualization tool that goes beyond simple charts and explores data relationships in depth.

5. **TIBCO Spotfire**:

   Spotfire's advanced features, including data wrangling, predictive analytics, and real-time data integration, make it ideal for experts working with complex data environments. It's particularly useful in industries like healthcare, finance, and manufacturing.

Learning Resources & Communities

Becoming proficient in data visualization requires more than just familiarity with the tools; it requires a constant engagement with learning and a deeper understanding of data science principles. Below are some top learning resources and communities for both beginners and experts:

Online Courses & Tutorials

1. **Coursera**:
   Coursera offers courses from top universities like the University of Washington and Johns Hopkins, covering topics like data visualization with R, data storytelling, and designing interactive dashboards.

2. **edX**:
   Like Coursera, edX hosts courses from major institutions such as MIT and Harvard, offering in-depth learning on data visualization using tools like Tableau, Power BI, and more.

3. **DataCamp**:
   DataCamp provides hands-on learning through interactive

exercises in R, Python, and other programming languages for data visualization. They offer a variety of courses ranging from beginner to advanced levels.

4. **Udemy**:

   Udemy's platform offers a wide range of affordable courses on data visualization, many of which are tailored to specific tools like Tableau, Power BI, and Python.

5. **YouTube**:

   YouTube is a valuable resource for free tutorials. Channels like "Data School" and "StatQuest" provide tutorials on data visualization and analysis with Python, R, and other tools.

Communities & Forums

1. **Reddit (r/dataisbeautiful)**:

   Reddit's DataIsBeautiful subreddit is a community where people share their data visualizations, receive feedback, and discuss best practices. It's a great place to get inspired and see the latest trends in data visualization.

2. **Stack Overflow**:

   Stack Overflow has a large community of developers and data scientists who can help answer questions and provide support on technical issues related to data visualization tools like D3.js, Plotly, and others.

3. **Tableau Community**:

   The Tableau Community offers forums, meetups, and live events where users can exchange tips, showcase visualizations, and learn about new features.

4. **Power BI Community**:

   The Power BI Community hosts forums, webinars, and learning resources for users at all levels, offering assistance with troubleshooting and advice from experienced Power BI users.

5. **Data Visualization Society**:

   The Data Visualization Society (DVS) is an international community of data visualization professionals and enthusiasts. Through online events, meetups, and a Slack group, DVS members can share ideas, learn from each other, and stay up to date with industry trends.

Data Sources for Practice & Inspiration

For any data visualization project, having the right dataset is key. Here are some top sources to find data to practice your skills and get inspiration for new visualizations:

1. **Kaggle**:

   Kaggle is one of the largest platforms for data science competitions and datasets. It offers thousands of free datasets on topics ranging from health to sports, business, and beyond.

2. **U.S. Government's Data.gov**:

   Data.gov is the U.S. government's open data repository. It provides access to datasets across various domains like agriculture, climate, and public safety.

3. **Google Public Data Explorer**:

   Google Public Data Explorer allows users to explore datasets from organizations like the World Bank and OECD, and easily create visualizations.

4. **FiveThirtyEight**:

   FiveThirtyEight offers a collection of datasets used in their data-driven articles, covering everything from politics to sports and economics. Their datasets are a great source of inspiration for journalists and analysts.

5. **World Bank Open Data**:

   The World Bank provides open access to global development data, which can be used for practicing visualizations around global issues like poverty, health, and education.

Conclusion

In this chapter, we've explored some of the best tools, learning resources, communities, and data sources for data visualization. Whether you're just getting started or are an expert looking to push your skills further, there's a wealth of resources available to help you bring your charts to life. By leveraging the right tools and continuously learning, you can transform raw data into visually compelling stories that inform, engage, and inspire.

Here are the links to the data visualization tools, learning resources, communities, and data sources mentioned:

Data Visualization Tools:

- **Google Data Studio**: https://datastudio.google.com/

- **Tableau Public**: https://public.tableau.com/

- **RAWGraphs**: https://rawgraphs.io/

- **Power BI Desktop**: https://powerbi.microsoft.com/desktop/

- **Plotly**: https://plotly.com/

- **Tableau**: https://www.tableau.com/

- **Qlik Sense**: https://www.qlik.com/products/qlik-sense

- **Sisense**: https://www.sisense.com/

- **TIBCO Spotfire**: https://www.tibco.com/products/tibco-spotfire

Learning Resources & Communities:

- **DataCamp**: https://www.datacamp.com/

- **Udemy**: https://www.udemy.com/

- **YouTube**: https://www.youtube.com/

- **Stack Overflow**: https://stackoverflow.com/

- **Kaggle**: https://www.kaggle.com/

- **Data Visualization Society**: https://www.datavisualizationsociety.com/

Data Sources for Practice & Inspiration:

- **Data.gov**: https://www.data.gov/

- **Google Public Data Explorer**: https://www.google.com/publicdata/directory

- **FiveThirtyEight Data**: https://data.fivethirtyeight.com/

- **World Bank Open Data**: https://data.worldbank.org/

CONCLUSION

Data visualization is an essential skill in today's data-driven world, providing the tools and techniques needed to transform raw data into meaningful insights. Throughout this book, we've covered the core principles and methods of creating effective and impactful visualizations. Here are some key takeaways:

- **Understanding Data**: The foundation of any great visualization is a deep understanding of the data you're working with. Knowing the type of data, the audience, and the insights you wish to convey is crucial for creating clear, relevant visuals.

- **Choosing the Right Visualization Type**: Different types of data require different visualization formats. We discussed bar charts, pie charts, line graphs, and advanced charts like heatmaps, scatter plots, and geospatial maps. Each has its strengths, and selecting the right one can make a huge difference in how your message is perceived.

- **Design Principles**: Simplicity and clarity are the heart of good design. We explored best practices such as minimizing chartjunk, avoiding misleading visuals, and using color and layout thoughtfully to ensure accessibility and readability.

- **Tools & Software**: We introduced both free and paid tools, from beginner-friendly platforms like Google Data Studio to more advanced software like Tableau and Qlik Sense. These tools empower you to create a wide range of visualizations, helping you effectively communicate your insights.

- **Learning & Growth**: Building your data visualization skills is an ongoing process. We highlighted resources, communities, and platforms that offer continuous learning opportunities, such as online courses, forums, and competitions like Kaggle.

Next Steps: Advancing Your Data Visualization Skills

Now that you have a solid foundation, it's time to take your data visualization skills to the next level. Here are some next steps to continue your journey:

1. **Practice Regularly**: The best way to hone your skills is through consistent practice. Take on new projects, whether through personal datasets, work-related challenges, or contributions to open-source projects. The

more data you visualize, the sharper your skills will become.

2. **Master Advanced Techniques**: As you gain confidence with basic charts, it's time to explore more sophisticated techniques like predictive modeling, interactive dashboards, and data-driven storytelling. Tools like Tableau and Power BI offer powerful features that can take your visualizations to the next level.

3. **Analyze Other Visualizations**: A great way to learn is by analyzing existing data visualizations. Look at case studies, industry reports, and design portfolios to see how other experts convey complex information. Analyze what works and what doesn't, and apply those insights to your own projects.

4. **Get Feedback**: Share your visualizations with others—whether they are colleagues, friends, or online communities—and get constructive feedback. Feedback helps you see blind spots and refine your approach, improving the overall impact of your work.

How to Keep Improving Your Visual Storytelling

Data visualization is about more than just creating beautiful charts—it's about telling a compelling story through data. To continue improving your visual storytelling abilities:

- **Focus on the Narrative**: Every visualization should tell a story. Ask yourself: What is the main takeaway I want the audience to have? What is the journey I want them to experience from start to finish? Ensure that your visualizations have a clear beginning, middle, and end.

- **Make Data Relatable**: The more relatable your data, the more powerful your visualization. Find ways to connect the data to real-world scenarios that your audience can understand and resonate with.

- **Embrace Simplicity**: As you gain experience, it may be tempting to create more complex visualizations. However, remember that simplicity is often more effective. Strive to create visualizations that convey information quickly and clearly, without overwhelming the audience.

- **Stay Curious and Evolve**: Data visualization is a rapidly evolving field. Stay up to date with new tools, techniques, and trends. Follow industry leaders, participate in webinars, and take advanced courses to keep pushing your boundaries.

In conclusion, data visualization is an art that requires a blend of technical skills, design thinking, and storytelling abilities. By continuously practicing, learning from others, and staying curious, you can create impactful visualizations that not only present data but also inspire action and drive understanding.

APPENDIX

Data Sources & Best Practices for Clean Data

One of the most important factors in creating effective visualizations is having clean, reliable data. Without proper data cleaning and preparation, even the most sophisticated visualization tools will not yield accurate insights. Below are some best practices for ensuring the data you use is clean and ready for visualization.

1. Data Collection

- **Source Reliability**: Always ensure your data is coming from a reliable and reputable source. Public datasets, like those from government websites, or commercial data platforms, tend to have higher credibility. For example, sites like Data.gov and Kaggle provide access to high-quality, well-documented datasets.

- **Data Validation**: Always validate your data before starting any analysis. Cross-check sources when possible, and ensure that it is up-to-date. Incomplete or outdated data can mislead your analysis and visuals.

2. Data Cleaning

- **Removing Duplicates**: Duplicates can significantly skew your results. Make sure you remove any repeated entries in your dataset before starting the visualization process.

- **Handling Missing Data**: Missing data is common in datasets and needs to be handled appropriately. You can either impute missing values with mean, median, or other suitable values, or you can remove rows with missing values depending on the analysis.

- **Standardizing Data**: Make sure all data is standardized for uniformity. For example, if you are working with dates, ensure they are formatted consistently (e.g., YYYY-MM-DD). Similarly, ensure that categories (like "Yes" or "No") are consistent across the dataset.

- **Outlier Detection**: Outliers are data points that differ significantly from other observations. While they can sometimes provide valuable insights, they can also distort analysis if not properly managed. It's important to decide how to handle outliers—whether to remove, adjust, or further investigate them.

- **Data Transformation**: When necessary, normalize or scale data to bring all variables onto a comparable scale.

This step ensures that no single variable dominates your analysis due to its scale.

3. Tools for Data Cleaning

- **OpenRefine**: A powerful tool for working with messy data, allowing you to clean, transform, and enrich data across large datasets. https://openrefine.org/

- **Trifacta Wrangler**: A tool that helps with data cleaning and transformation, especially for large datasets. It offers both free and paid versions. https://www.trifacta.com/

Reference Charts for Choosing the Right Visualization

Selecting the right type of chart can make or break a visualization. Here are some general guidelines and a reference chart to help you choose the best visualization based on your data:

Data Type	Visualization Type	When to Use
Single Variable (Quantitative)	Bar chart, Histogram, Pie	To show distribution or frequency of a

Data Type	Visualization Type	When to Use
	chart	single variable.
Two Variables (Quantitative)	Scatter plot, Line graph	To show relationships, trends, or correlations.
Categorical Data	Bar chart, Pie chart	To compare different categories or proportions.
Time Series Data	Line chart, Area chart	To visualize data over time or trends.
Geospatial Data	Map (Choropleth,	To show location-based data or spatial

Data Type	Visualization Type	When to Use
	Bubble map)	distributions.
Part-to-Whole Relationships	Stacked bar chart, Pie chart	To compare parts of a whole (ensure clarity).
Multi-Variable Data	Heatmap, Bubble chart, Radar chart	To explore correlations or patterns across multiple variables.
Hierarchical Data	Tree map, Sunburst chart, Dendrogram	To represent hierarchical or nested structures.

Each type of visualization is designed to communicate different insights. The choice depends on the relationship between the data points and the message you wish to convey.

Additional Reading & Online Courses

To further expand your knowledge in data visualization and to keep up with new trends and technologies, here are some books and online courses you might find helpful:

Books:

- **"The Visual Display of Quantitative Information" by Edward Tufte**
  A classic in the field, Tufte's book is often considered the foundation for anyone interested in the principles of data visualization. It teaches how to display data in an accurate, insightful, and engaging way.

- **"Storytelling with Data: A Data Visualization Guide for Business Professionals" by Cole Nussbaumer Knaflic**
  This book teaches how to tell compelling stories with data through effective visualizations. It's great for beginners and intermediate data professionals looking to connect with their audience more effectively.

- **"Data Visualization: A Practical Introduction" by Kieran Healy**

  A more technical read that covers both theory and practical implementation of data visualizations. It's perfect for anyone interested in learning about the tools and principles behind successful data visualizations.

Online Courses:

- **Coursera – Data Visualization with Tableau**

  Offered by the University of California, Davis, this course teaches how to use Tableau for creating advanced visualizations. It's ideal for both beginners and intermediate users.

  https://www.coursera.org/learn/data-visualization-with-tableau

- **Udemy – Data Visualization in Excel for Beginners**

  A great entry-level course that focuses on using Excel's built-in tools for creating professional-grade charts and graphs.

  https://www.udemy.com/course/data-visualization-in-excel-for-beginners/

- **LinkedIn Learning – Learning Data Visualization**

  A comprehensive course that covers the fundamentals of

data visualization, including data storytelling, selecting the right charts, and using software like Tableau and Power BI.

https://www.linkedin.com/learning/learning-data-visualization

- **DataCamp – Introduction to Data Visualization with Python**
  This course teaches how to visualize data using Python libraries like Matplotlib and Seaborn. It's perfect for those looking to apply data visualization within a coding environment.
  https://www.datacamp.com/courses/introduction-to-data-visualization-with-python

- **edX – Data Science and Machine Learning for Public Policy: Data Visualization**
  This course from the University of California, Berkeley, focuses on using data visualization to convey complex data in the context of public policy.
  https://www.edx.org/course/data-science-and-machine-learning-for-public-policy-data-visualization

This appendix provides you with valuable resources to enhance your data visualization skills, ensuring that your journey toward becoming a skilled data storyteller continues smoothly. Whether you're cleaning data, selecting the right chart, or exploring further learning materials, the tools and resources here will empower you to refine your visual storytelling and produce meaningful, insightful visualizations.

REFERENCES

1. Tufte, Edward R. *The Visual Display of Quantitative Information*. Graphics Press, 2001.

2. Knaflic, Cole Nussbaumer. *Storytelling with Data: A Data Visualization Guide for Business Professionals*. Wiley, 2015.

3. Healy, Kieran. *Data Visualization: A Practical Introduction*. Princeton University Press, 2018.

4. Everhart, Nathan. "Data Cleaning: A Practical Guide to Data Preparation." *Data Science Review*, 2020, https://www.datasciencereview.com/data-cleaning-practical-guide.

5. "Top 10 Best Free Data Visualization Tools in 2025." *Tech Radar*, 2025, https://www.techradar.com/best/data-visualization-tools.

6. "Data Visualization with Tableau." Coursera, University of California, Davis, https://www.coursera.org/learn/data-visualization-with-tableau.

7. McKinney, Wes. *Python for Data Analysis*. O'Reilly Media, 2018.

8. "Visualizing Data: A Practical Guide to Data Visualization Techniques." *Kaggle*, 2023, https://www.kaggle.com/learn/visualizing-data.

9. "Interactive Data Visualization with D3.js." *DataCamp*, 2025, https://www.datacamp.com/courses/interactive-data-visualization-with-d3.

10. "The Power of Data Visualization in Decision-Making." *Harvard Business Review*, 2024, https://hbr.org/2024/04/the-power-of-data-visualization-in-decision-making.

11. "Introduction to Data Visualization with Python." *DataCamp*, 2023, https://www.datacamp.com/courses/introduction-to-data-visualization-with-python.

12. "Choosing the Right Data Visualization for Your Data." *Visualizing Data*, https://www.visualizingdata.com.

13. "Data Visualization Best Practices." *Tableau*, https://www.tableau.com/learn/articles/data-visualization-best-practices.

14. "Storytelling with Data: Best Practices for Data Visualization." *LinkedIn Learning*, 2025, https://www.linkedin.com/learning/learning-data-visualization.

15. "A Beginner's Guide to Data Visualization: Tips and Tools for Success." *Google Data Studio Blog*, 2024, https://www.blog.google/.

These references provide a range of resources from foundational books to current online tools and courses, ensuring that readers can continue learning and refining their data visualization skills. Whether you are a beginner or an expert, these works will offer valuable insights and practical guidance to help you master the art of data visualization.